The Aquinas Lecture, 1956

THE TRUTH
THAT FREES

Under the Auspices of the Aristotelian Society
of Marquette University

By

GERARD SMITH, S.J., Ph.D.

D1248864

MARQUETTE UNIVERSITY PRESS
MILWAUKEE
1956

Nihil Obstat

    Francis C. Wade, S.J., censor deputatus
    Milwaukiae, die 27 mensis Februarii, 1956

Imprimatur

    ✠Albertus G. Meyer
    Archiepiscopus Milwaukiensis
    Milwaukiae, die 28 mensis Februarii, 1956

Imprimi Potest

    Leo J. Burns, S.J.
    Praepositus Provincialis Provinciae Wisconsiensis
    Milwaukiae, die 27 mensis Februarii, 1956

Prefatory

The Aristotelian Society of Marquette University each year invites a scholar to deliver a lecture in honor of St. Thomas Aquinas. Customarily delivered on the Sunday nearest March 7, the feast day of the Society's patron saint, these lectures are called the Aquinas lectures.

In 1956 — the year of the University's 75th Anniversary — the Academic Vice-President of the University suggested that the Aristotelian Society invite the director of the Marquette department of philosophy, Fr. Gerard Smith, S.J., to deliver the lecture. The Society now has the pleasure of recording that lecture, given March 18 in the Brooks Memorial Union.

Father Smith was born April 25, 1896 at Sioux City, Iowa. He took his A.B. at St. Louis University in 1919 and his A.M. in 1921. He studied at Ore Place, Hastings, England, at Fourvière, Lyons, France and at the Pontifical Institute of Mediaeval Studies at the University of Toronto where he received his Ph.D. in 1936.

He was ordained a Jesuit priest in Dublin, Ireland, in 1927.

Fr. Smith was an instructor at St. Ignatius High School and Loyola University, Chicago, 1921-24. He was head of the religion department, Marquette University, 1929-30, and instructor and associate professor of philosophy at Marquette, 1931-34, acting as regent of the School of Business Administration, 1933-34. He was associate professor of philosophy at St. Louis University, 1936-37, returned to Marquette as associate professor, 1937-45, was made professor of philosophy in 1945 and has been head of the department of philosophy since 1947.

He was president of the American Catholic Philosophical Association, 1950-51. In 1955 he was awarded the Spellman Aquinas Medal by the Association.

Father Smith is the author of *Natural Theology* (Macmillan, N.Y., 1951). His dissertation was *Molina and Liberty* (U. of Toronto, 1936).

He was editor of *Jesuit Thinkers of the Renaissance*, essays presented to Fr. John F. McCormick, S.J., by his students (Marquette University Press, Milwaukee, 1939) and of four numbers of the *Highway to Heaven Series* (Bruce, Milwaukee): *Life of the Soul* (1933), *The Mass* (1936), and *Highway to God* (1942).

He is editor of the Aquinas Lecture series, and chairman of the editorial board of the *Mediaeval Philosophical Texts in Translation*, published by the Marquette University Press.

He is also a member of the board of editors of the Christian Wisdom Series (Macmillan, N.Y.).

Father Smith is the author of a large number of reviews, a long list of public addresses and lectures, and the following articles:

"Avicenna and the Possibles," *New Scholasticism*, XVII (Oct., 1943) 340-357; also in *Essays in Modern Scholasticism*, in

Honor of John F. McCormick, S.J., 1874-1943, edited by Anton C. Pegis. (Newman Bookshop, Westminster, Md., 1944), pp. 116-133.

"Before You Start Talking About God; Metaphysical and Epistemological Doctrines of Being," *Modern Schoolman*, XXIII (Nov., 1945) 24-43.

"Bosanquet and the Concrete Universal," *Proceedings of the Missouri Academy of Science*, 1937.

"Concept in St. Thomas, The," *Modern Schoolman*, XV (March, 1938) pp. 52-56.

"Date in the History of Epistemology, A," *Thomist*, V (Jan., 1943) pp. 246-255; also in *The Maritain Volume of the Thomist*, (Sheed and Ward, New York, 1943).

"Historical Approach to Philosophy, The," *Proceedings of the Jesuit Philosophical Association*, 1937, p. 7.

"Intelligence and Liberty," *Proceedings of the American Catholic Philosophical Association*, XVI (1940) pp. 69-85; also in *New Scholasticism* XV (Jan., 1941) 1-17.

"Kant's Epistemology," *Modern Schoolman*, XI (Nov., 1933) pp. 3-4, 6, 19-20.

"Kant's Ethics," *Modern Schoolman*, XI (Jan., 1934) pp. 27-28, 30, 45.

"Law, an Affair of Reason," *Modern Schoolman*, XVII (Nov., 1939) pp. 2-4, 8-9.

"Luther and Free Choice," *Modern Schoolman*, XX (Jan., 1943) pp. 78-88.

"Metaphysics and Logic," *Proceedings of the American Catholic Philosophical Association*, XIII (1937) pp. 173-175.

"Mr. Adler and the Order of Learning," *Proceedings of the National Catholic Educational Association*, XVIII (1942) pp. 140-162; also in *Jesuit Educational Quarterly*, VI (Mar., 1944) pp. 205-221.

"Nature and Uses of Liberty," *New Scholasticism*, XXVI (1952) pp. 305-326.

"Natural End of Man, The," *Proceedings of the American Catholic Philosophical Association*, XXIII (1949) pp. 47-61.

"New English St. Thomas," *Thought* XX (June, 1945) pp. 212-216 (Review of

Basic Writings of St. Thomas by Anton C. Pegis).

"Note on Predication," *New Scholasticism*, XV (July, 1941) pp. 222-237.

"Note on the Teaching of Philosophy, A," (Anonymous), *Jesuit Educational Quarterly*, IV (Dec., 1941) pp. 120-122.

"Philosophy and Man's Unity in the Ultimate End," *Proceedings of the American Catholic Philosophical Association*, XXVII (April, 1953) pp. 60-83.

"Position of Philosophy in a Catholic School," *Proceedings of the American Catholic Philosophical Association*, XXIX (1955) pp. 20-40.

"Query on the Natural End of Man," *Modern Schoolman*, XXV (Nov., 1947) p. 38.

"Reflection on the Nature of Man and the A-Bomb," *Proceedings of the American Catholic Philosophical Association*, XIV (1951) pp. 11-16.

"Reverend John F. McCormick, S.J.— A Tribute," *Proceedings of the American*

Catholic Philosophical Association, XIX (1943) pp. 1-5.

"Science and Philosophy," *The Biologist,* XXXV (1953) pp. 72-80.

To the list of his writings the Aristotelian Society has the pleasure of adding *The Truth That Frees.*

The Truth That Frees

I propose to suggest an answer to this question: What is the truth which sets men free? The precedent for fixing in some way the theme of our 75th anniversary, "the pursuit of truth to make men free," has already been set. On June 1, 1955, Fr. Edward J. Drummond, S.J., did an excellent job in explaining to the faculty, term by term, what our theme meant.[1] His was a homily on the complete text. My remarks will concern a part of the text, the relation of freedom to truth.

I

We may begin the answer to our question with a couple of simple and obvious examples of truths which set men free.

That penicillin often cures pneumonia is a truth which often frees men from pneumonia. That a circular body rotating on its axis causes less friction when in contact with other surfaces than were it not circular and not rotating is a truth which gave men the wheel, and thus freed them from the necessity of dragging burdens, including themselves, upon sleds or upon the bare ground.

The first thing we may notice about such truths seems to be this: they are profitless unless we know them. No doubt penicillin could always have cured pneumonia, but that truth never helped us — even though Galen did think highly of mold — until we knew it.

That we must know the truth if it is to set us free points to a highly intelligible and therefore mysterious situation which can be described in the light of two curt

remarks directed by Aristotle to the Sophists. Aristotle says that the truth of the
proposition (supposed true), "you are
pale," is not in this, that we truly think
that you are pale; rather, it is because you
are pale that we who say this have the
truth.[2] The truth, he is saying, exists in
two situations: first, in the situation of
being a state of affairs, whether one knows
that state of affairs or not, e.g., the truth
lies in your being pale; secondly, the truth
lies in the situation of our knowing a state
of affairs, e.g., in our knowing you are pale.
The two situations are so related that the
truth of your being pale can cause the truth
of our knowledge that you are pale, but not
the other way about: knowledge, true or
false, that you are pale cannot cause you to
be pale. No one is pale because he thinks
so; rather, one is right in thinking he is pale
only when and because he is pale.[3]

A great thinker is never satisfied with
disposing of an adversary. His greatness is
measured also by his success in unmasking
and if possible destroying his adversary's
latent and basic prejudice. Aristotle's second remark unmasks the Sophist's latent
prejudice. He says, "it is impossible for
anything at the same time to be and not to
be . . . It is, then, impossible that it should
be at the same time true to say of the same
thing that it is a man and is not a man."[4]
Let us set this statement of Aristotle's in
the context of one of St. Thomas Aquinas'
commentaries on it.[5] Assume false silver or
gold, or as we should say, counterfeit.
Counterfeit gold is, nevertheless, true lead.
In other words, there is a state of affairs in
the instance "lead," which is true whether
one thinks that lead is gold or not, and it is
this state of affairs which Sophists are
denying when they say that truth resides

only in thought. Sophists think that the
truth depends only upon the way we look
at things. Although not denying that the
truth of the way you look at things lies in
the way you look at things — where else
could the truth of thought reside except
in thought — Aristotle and St. Thomas
Aquinas maintain that over and above the
truth of thought there is a truth of things:
lead is lead, whether it counterfeit gold
or not, and this is what the Sophists are
either denying or professing not to know.
As men who can't read or won't are pretty
much in the same boat — there is nothing
for them to read, so for Sophists, who pro-
fess that they can't know or who refuse to
know, there is nothing to know.

Can the *a priori* conviction of the Sophists be destroyed as well as unmasked?
Not if it be opposed only by another prejudice equally *a priori*. Sophism maintains

that this is so. That there is the truth of things is for the Sophists no less a prejudice of Aristotelian realism than is their own conviction that there is no truth of things. Nevertheless, prejudice for prejudice, Aristotle's realism has this in its favor; counterfeit gold will not bear examination; under scrutiny it will appear for what it is, viz., lead. Call this a prejudice if you will, but it is at least a prejudice which experience can check. On the other hand, the Sophists' prejudice that the truth lies wholly in the way we look at things leaves us nothing at all to check except the way we look at things. This, according to Aristotle is next to intellectual suicide — the life of a polyp, as he says with gay contempt,[6] because men for one reason or another often think up states of affairs which are not so, e.g., that counterfeit lead is good gold, and how is their thought to be tested if there be no lead or gold to test their thought against?

We may conclude that the truth, which sets men free, lies both in thought and things, and if there be error, that can reside only in thought, never in things. With this conclusion we may now face, without evading it, this issue: what is the state of affairs which if we but knew it would set us free?

Whether with William James we describe our infantile impression of the world about us as "one big blooming buzzing Confusion," or whether with Aristotle we describe those impressions, infantile or not, as a rout in battle,[7] in either case there doesn't seem to be anything about us which holds steady long enough for us to identify it as being the same thing the next time we take a look at it. One of Shakespeare's characters muses "they say the owl was a baker's daughter." It could be. The world of becoming and generation, like angle-worms in a can, is a twisting, coiling, slippery, weltering mass of stuff whose second description is never quite the same as its first. A rout in battle indeed where no man makes a stand.

Yet all is not lost. The rout "is stopped," Aristotle says, "first by one man making a stand and then another, until the original formation has been restored."[8] "Let us now restate," he goes on, "the account already given, though with insufficient clearness." (He refers to the account just given, the rout in battle being stopped by one man, etc.) He now states, this time presumably with sufficient clearness, what he means. "When one of a number of logically indiscriminable particulars has made a stand [as thus, this and that man, though logically indiscriminable as being men, both make a stand by both being men and not, say, fish], the earliest universal is present in the soul; for though the act of sense-perception is of the particular, its content is universal — is man, for example, not the man Callias. A fresh stand is made among these rudimentary universals, and the process does not cease until the indivisible concepts, the true universals [these are the categories], are established, e.g., such and such a species of animal is a step towards the genus animal, which by the same process is a step towards a further generalization" [e.g., towards living, body, substance].[9] It would be impossible indeed to state the matter with more sufficient clearness, though a paraphrase of Aristotle's statement might be useful.

There are fixed states of affairs, islets of intellectual safety in a flux of change, footholds upon slippery terrain, viewpoints which are invariable. Whenever a man understands what the necessary features of any situation are, his knowledge has made a stand, because the situation itself has made a stand. Assume, e.g., two top flight chess players before a chess problem which has only one solution. They will both come up with the same solution, and so will all the kibitzers who are of the same calibre as they. Should the problem have several possible solutions, everyone in the party will proffer the same several possible solutions, and there never were, are, or will be any other possible solution or solutions to the given problem. Such are universals: viewpoints which disregard the unessential, the non-necessary features of any situation, e.g., that a chess game is being played by Russians, with ivory chessmen, etc., etc., and which are grasps of only those features of a situation without which the situation would not be the situation it is, in the instance the chess problem and its solution. Should the solution or solutions of an identical problem vary to the point of contrariety or contradiction, that would only mean that someone was wrong. The universally intelligible features of any situation do not vary, not unless the universal situation itself varies, and then we have a new universal.[10]

What keeps us from always recognizing that the universally intelligible features of a situation are absolutely and necessarily invariable is this: the sensible features of many situations often do not vary much either; they too are often stable and necessary, but only up to a point. And so we tend to confuse the absolutely necessary or universal features of an intelligible situation with the relatively necessary features of a sensible situation. Assume, for example, a spherical body ever so slightly squashed, to the point, say, of being eccentric by 1/100,000,000 mm. No one could recognize the sensible difference between the perfect and the slightly squashed sphere, because there isn't any macroscopic sensible difference between the two. Yet there is an intelligible difference, and we so clearly recognize this that we would only stare at the lout who denied the difference between the perfect and imperfect sphere even though neither he nor we could see the difference with our eyes. The fact is, there is more in the perfect sphere than meets the eye. It is so with all universals. We do not see them with the eyes of the body; we see them only with the eyes of our mind.

We must look at this more closely. Even if we could put the slightly squashed sphere under a microscope and see that it is squashed, still and all, no instrument whatsoever can measure with absolute accuracy the actual dimensions of any sphere at all, squashed or not. Everything keeps on bulging or contracting. Nor can the actual speed, place, or position of anything whatsoever be measured with absolute accuracy. Light, for one thing, disturbs everything we measure, so that the size, place, and speed of things are retrospective measurements of them: they are the size, place, and speed which things would have had if we had not joggled them by the light from our measuring instruments. But there's more to it than that. Not only can we not measure things with absolute accuracy because our measuring instruments joggle them: it is not even true that, even if we didn't joggle them, things have absolute quantities. See well what this means. It means that absolute quantities are not in things at all, that the supposed absolute quantities in things cannot be measured, not because they are there though too tiny to be measured, but because they are not in things at all. The mathematical universal *qua* universal is not only not sensible at all, it cannot even be sensible. It is only intelligible.

The same goes for the universals revealed by sensation. The hot, the cold, the soft, the hard, the sour, the sweet, bones, flesh, and so on, these *qua* universals are not in things at all. They are only in the mind. Like "mathematicals," "physicals" *qua* universals cannot be in things. Fancy "the hot" existing but not in anything which *is* hot!

What, then, and why do we learn about things in terms of their mathematical and physical predicates? What we learn is clear enough. We learn their universal features which these predicates disclose, e.g., we learn about X that he is a good tailor, and his prices are right. Why we learn is more difficult to state, and for this reason: things are *not* their universal features (X is *a* good tailor, not "good tailor"); yet their universal features are true of things (X *is* a good tailor all the same). A seeming contradiction in terms. For, if a universal be in things, it is not universal; and if a universal be not in things, it cannot be true of them.

This apparent contradiction can be resolved only if each thing be a composite of two components, neither of which is a thing, but by which two components each thing exists. This will mean that things have in them a factor not disclosed by the universal, a factor which is not a universally intelligible structure, not an essence; and it will also mean that this factor in things, which is not universal, not a universally intelligible structure, not an essence, is the very factor which affects the universal with *that* factor's coefficient of contingency and of non-universality, but which nevertheless leaves the universal untouched in *its* status of universality and necessity. Conversely, if that factor affects the universal with its own contingency, it itself is also affected by the *universal's* necessity, but not upon the score of its *own* contingency. Thus things have both universal and contingent predicates. Though it be not necessary that Socrates run, nevertheless if he does run, run he must.[11] If any difficulty over the matter persists, that will be because we have forgotten to think of the universally intelligible structure of things and of the factor just mentioned as the components of a being; we have begun to think of each component as a being. Man, the universal, does not exist, but *a* man exists, and the existent man has two features to him: a *man* feature, and the factor by which that *man* feature exists with all the vicissitudes which his status as an existent man demands, but with no vicissitudes at all so far forth as his being man is concerned. The baby and adult baby, viz., the man, are unquestionably the same in their universally intelligible man structure, and as unquestionably that man structure is a structure of one who changes. All this is so because it is he, the man, who changes, because it is he, the man, who exists; it is not the necessary features of the man structure which change or exist. A man exists, not his structure; nor does he exist apart from his structure.

We are here faced with a profound mystery. There is in things a factor not disclosed by the universal predicates of things. That factor it is which gives to things both their necessary and contingent intelligible structure in existence, and so it is the structure in existence which is at once both necessary and contingent.

The time has come to speak of that factor. Two things must be said about it, and the first thing was said by Aristotle, the second by St. Thomas Aquinas.

Aristotle said that it is a subject of predicates which is never a predicate.[12] For example, let sulphur be described by the following admixture of mathematical and physical predicates: a non-metallic yellowish element; atomic weight, 32.066; fusion point, 113° centigrade; boiling point, 444.53°; combustion point in air, 360°; in oxygen, 280°, etc. There is enough here to enable anyone to recognize sulphur anywhere. Now assume a man who claims to have found a sample of sulphur which does not have some or all of these predicates. Crazy, we'd call him, for these predicates are parts of the definition of sulphur. Yet the only reason why these predicates are parts of the definition of sulphur is because they assume a "clunk" which is not its definition or any part of its definition. If all these predicates did not assume such a "clunk," they would be saying that what has an atomic weight of 32.066 has an atomic weight of 32.066, a no more revelatory bit of information than that a black cat is black. Worse, it is saying "black cat" twice, as if the second dictum added a jot to the first. In other words, if we refuse to recognize that there is a subject which is always implied but never fully disclosed by universal predicates, then these predicates are falling like hailstones upon nothing. The subject has disappeared and we are no longer talking about anything.[13] Mathematical and physical predicates surround a subject like a sack and we walk off with the sack and the subject in it, quite justifiably content that we have trapped something in the sack, without, for all that, knowing fully what it is which is in the sack except in terms of its mathematical and physical predicates. And so we must know that the subject is *not* its predicates if we are not to say the same thing about it twice over. Call a thing any name it deserves, but don't forget that there is something you are naming which is not the mathematical and physical names you give it. Otherwise you couldn't say a *man is fat,* but only *fat is fat.* Indeed you couldn't even say *fat is fat;* you could only say *fat* twice, and then there would be no one left to *be* fat, not even "fat," for surely "fat" cannot exist; only fat men exist. Mathematical and physical predicates always describe something which they can only imply. They can do no more.[14]

II

Can more be done? Can we reap more knowledge about things than the harvest which their mathematical quantities and sensible qualities yield? Is there a state of affairs, an intelligible structure to things which can be more fully disclosed than by their mathematical and physical predicates? There is if we raise our sights above the level of mathematics and the physics of nature. It is one of Aristotle's glories to have seen this. There is, to repeat after Aristotle, a subject of predicates which is never a predicate.[15] This subject Aristotle named substance, and we must now see better what he meant by substance.

If we grant as evident that something

exists, it is self-evident that there must be a proper subject of the verb and of the situation described by the verb "exists." Men are not made up of little men, nor houses of little houses.[16] Understand this remark thus: if you explode a man into pieces, none of his pieces is a man. Now strengthen that insight with this one: an army will disperse into many men, but an army is not the proper subject of existence. Only each individual in the army is such a subject. Finally, see that even if a man were made up of little men, then each little man would have to be, in turn, made up of still littler men, and these last of still littler men, and so on *ad infinitum* — until either nothing exists, because there is no proper subject of existence, or else, if something does exist, we can never know that it does. This is sheer disaster to knowledge and to things. Disaster to things, because if things

are only aggregates, then not even the aggregates exist, for they too are aggregates
ad indefinitum, and thus there is nothing.
Imagine an aggregate of things with no
things to be an aggregate of![17] Disaster to
knowledge, because if knowledge knows
only aggregates, it never knows what they
are aggregates of, and so knowledge cannot even know aggregates.

Profound, almost miraculous in fact,
was Aristotle's insight that the pedestal of
material reality is substance, the subject of
which you say "it exists." Profounder still
was St. Thomas Aquinas' insight that any
substance we experience is other than its
act of existing. If sheer intellect could
come as far as to see that the heart of
reality is substance, any deeper insight
into substance must have somehow been
guided and sustained by a different light.

So it was. "In the beginning God

created heaven and earth." So within the history of Christian thought St. Thomas Aquinas came to think that even substance did not exist because it was the proper subject of the situation we describe by the verb "exists"; rather, so revelation led St. Thomas to think, because a substance existed, this is the reason why it is the proper subject of the situation described by the verb "exists." This was a Christian deepening of Greek philosophy itself.

Impossible though it be to communicate here and now all the implications of St. Thomas' insight, I must at least try to describe the insight itself.

There is something about substance as we experience it which makes it impossible for the human mind not only to identify it with its mathematical and physical predicates, as Aristotle saw, but also impossible to identify it with its status of being an existent, as only Christians saw. Assume an existent: you, with your ears laid back, and eating corn off the cob. Assume, same props, your dinner partner. You cannot both have the identical status of being an existent, else you would both be one existent. This is against the fact, for there are two of you. Nor can even one of you be identified with the status of being an existent, for then there would not be enough in that status to cover the situation of the other fellow, for he too is an existent. There must, in other words, be enough in the status of being an existent to cover the situation of both of you. Since there is enough, each of you shares in the same status, yet not so as to cause you to be one half an existent or a fraction thereof and him to be another half an existent or a fraction thereof. Imagine an existent which one half is and one half isn't! Each of you shares in the same status in the sense that each of you fully exists, yet, because there are two of you who so share, neither of you is identically that status. The same goes for all experienced existents: none is identical with the status of existing, which it enjoys.

Such being the situation, the following question, as Leibniz saw,[18] becomes highly pertinent; why do you exist? Pertinent, because there being no identity between you and the status of existing which you enjoy, there is no necessity that you be at all. Why, then, do you exist?

It is unnecessary to tell this audience that the Christian answer to that question is this: you were created.

Let us now direct our attention to the relevance of all this to the matter of the "truth which sets us free." Recall that truth resides in things and, if known, in the mind. Recall that it is only in knowing the truth of things that we can be free. What, then, is the truth of things which if known can set us free? That truth of things is 1) their intelligible structures, revealed by the universals of their mathematical and physical predicates; 2) that truth of things is their situation of being substances, or proper subjects of existing, which situation, because 3) it is not identical with the act of existing of any experienced substance, is a created situation. Let us for the sake of the record remember that the Greeks made the first two points and Christians made the third.

And now to freedom. Be it noted, of course, that freedom is a dominion which includes knowledge. Knowledge is enlarged rather than diminished by such inclusion; but if we are to get precisely at the relation of truth to freedom, we must now ask: what happens when the state of affairs or the truth of things just described gets into the mind, what happens, i.e., when we *know* all this?

First, when we know mathematicals and physicals, we know "ways out." If you "want out," you can get out only if there are ways out, and you know them. Suppose, for example, you wish to get from Milwaukee to Chicago. If there is no way, or if there is but you don't know it, you can't go. If there is only one way, and you know it, you can take only one way. If you know several ways, you can in principle take any of them. These "ways out" are the universals, rudimentary at first but increasing in precision and variety. Thus, if you know the universals in a wheel, you can travel much faster than on Shank's mares. If you know the universals of aero- and thermodynamics, you can get there very fast indeed, and if you know the universals of nuclear physics you can, I suppose, get there as fast as you can be blown there.

See well the sort of liberty which the knowledge of universals provides. A man who is pushed hard enough will fall. This is the compulsion or necessity of nature. But a man who knows the universal of side-stepping need not fall at all, because he knows how to side-step. We are in a situation, when we know universals, which is quite different from the situation of a nature, which knows nothing. A nature, like a tree, can only grow. A man who knows a tree can crossbreed it, replant it in another lot, kill it, or make it flourish, and so on. A tree can't do any of these things of itself, for it doesn't know how to. We know how. Is the truth of these sorts of know-how, these universals, a source of liberty? It is. Yet there are limits to this sort of know-how, and so there are limits to the sort of liberty the know-how gives us. The universal limits our knowledge, first, by as much as one necessary situation is not another. To know the cause of small-pox is not to know the cause of cancer, and so we are free to cure or immunize against smallpox, but not, with the same success, cancer. Secondly, the universal puts limits upon our liberty by as much as it confines our knowledge and therefore our freedom to the area of material substances. In other words, even if we knew all the neces-sary situations of all the material sub-stances there are, we would be free only to dicker better with the world, free only to drive a more advantageous bargain with our environment, free only to better and to pass on to others our situation *vis à vis* the forces of nature. An excellent freedom no doubt, but it is not enough.

In order to see that it is not enough, let us go straight to the crucial case. Nobody knows how or can know how to avoid death. True, we can delay death, and perhaps to a far greater extent than we know how to right now. Yet there is no escaping death, because the universal of the "corruptible body" is the source of the universal proposition "it is appointed for all men once to die."

Seize well this situation. Two plus two are four. Nobody asked us about that. We have to accept it. You can't nail jelly to the wall, babies can't spit straight (because they can't spit at all), etc. Nobody asked us about all that either. We must take nature as we find it. Her laws are our laws. When you butt into a wall, can you, after you have butted it, cause yourself not to have butted it, or cause the wall you butted not to have been a wall, or cause a door to have been the very spot in the wall which you butted? Of course not. Wise men quit butting, or make a door, or retire in good order. This is the only liberty they have when confronted by necessary situations in nature. And if science deals only with necessary situations in nature, as it does, the picture of the world which positivistic science presents is simply this: whereas we can for a while pick among and combine the universals which science proffers, the time comes when we must willy-nilly quit our antics and die. Thus the final word of positivistic science seems to be that man is but a key on a keyboard, and the tune played thereon is in the last analysis played by nature.[19]

I am far from decrying the situation in which science leaves us. A man would be a fool not to enjoy the advantages which science offers. Bigger and better gadgets.

By all means. To move bigger and bigger
bodies farther and faster. Excellent. To
probe even into the nature of a human
spirit, and to see there at its heart the faint
analogate of the mystery of mysteries,
which is the Fatherhood of God, and in
which Freud in his less happy moments
saw, alas, only sex — all this is to the good.
Indeed all this is to the good in a way not
dreamt of by positivism. Positivism must
think that a scientist's occupation is trif-
ling, because it must think that his science
will all end one day, because it thinks that
the ganglion or bit of mold which is the
scientist will eventually cease to be. Christianity, however, has a higher estimate of
a scientist and his science. In Christianity
science exists within the liberty of a scientist, and it will exist there forever, because
a scientist will exist forever. In the positivistic vision of science, however, man's only

liberty is to put off for a while the inevitable, to play a losing game, to caper a while upon this earth before he, together with his scientific antics, falls flat on his face there to lie forever.

Can we accept positivism's version of the matter as the last word? Many men do not. Many men have not. This is sufficient to show us that men need not leave themselves with a knowledge which is no more than a progressively more perfect knowledge of universals. Aristotle did not wish to be left with such knowledge: "we must not listen to those," he said, "who advise us, being mortal, to think on mortal things."[20] Socrates himself, after a long lifetime spent in the pursuit of the knowledge of universals, had another knowledge. He asserted it boldly: "no harm can come to the good man in this life or the next."[21] Note Socrates' personal situation

carefully. Here is a man who is quite sure
that he is facing death, and soon. Christians, of course, are in a privileged situation in the face of death. Christians have
heard the words, "I am the Resurrection
and the Life; he who believes in me will
live, even if he dies; and no one that lives
and believes in me shall die forever."[22]
Christians hope one day to hear the same
words, and spoken with the same accent,
which our Lord addressed to the dead little
daughter of anguished parents, "honey, get
up" (*Talitha, kumi*), or these words addressed to one four days dead, "Lazarus,
come forth." The source of Christians'
hope is the One Who said "I will rise again
on the third day," and did.

III

If there be any state of affairs the
knowledge of which is the source of a

liberty over and above our liberty to take ways out, this is it. For this situation in which man can and does make the most and the best of his good knowledge of universals is when known not a way out at all. If we name it plainly, it is rather a way into something, a way into eternal life. Our attention is still directed to knowledge situations. The question we must now face, however, is this: what is the way into eternal life? for it is only in knowing that way that our liberty to take it lies.

Before I suggest an answer, it must be remarked that no one need take the way into eternal life because he had heard from me or anyone else the description of that way. To know the way into eternal life by knowing the description of it is like knowing a country from knowing the map of the country. Now surely, to know a country from having known its map is not the same as to know it from having lived in it. Just so, to know the way into eternal life from having heard someone talk about it is not to live eternally. To live in a country one must move into it, dwell there. So here, to live eternally is to know eternal life by way of having occupied the region where those dwell who live forever. To live forever is to decide to become a citizen of the kingdom of God, and one becomes a citizen of the kingdom of God by deciding to live forever. I shall return to this point.

As we saw, when confronted with necessary situations in nature, we can pick and choose among them. We are not free to change the situations themselves, but only to thread our way among them. Involved in this free posture of ours before necessary situations in nature, the posture, namely, of one who can hew his way this way and that because he knows how to, there is a more mysterious posture still. To this more mysterious posture which is involved even in our attitude before necessary situations in nature, I now direct your attention, because it is there if anywhere that we shall find our liberty to live forever. Let me remind you once more that to find the spot of this our greatest liberty of all, the liberty to live forever, is not forwith to live forever. We must occupy that spot.

But, first, we must find it. A man who knows how to blow up the planet is surely freer in principle to blow it up than one who does not know. So too a man who knows several ways to blow it up is surely freer than one who knows only one way. This we have seen. Now, assume such a man. Ask him, do you propose to blow up the planet or not? He answers, $E = mc^2$. You are not answered. He is telling you

the formula, the universal, the recipe for
blowing us all to bits. He is not telling you
whether he proposes to do so or not. Thus,
within our liberty to take any of the various ways out which our knowledge suggests, there is also our liberty to take any
or not to take any way out which our
knowledge suggests. It is in this phase of
our liberty, called the liberty to use or to
exercise our knowledge or to refrain there-
from, that we must find, or not at all, our
liberty to live forever.[23]

A man who decides to make bad use
of his knowledge by, e.g., blowing up the
planet, suffers an evil which does not lie
wholly in the fact that he is blown up
along with the planet; and the man who
decides not to blow us all up enjoys a
good which does not lie wholly in living
out his days serenely upon mother earth.
Obviously it is bad to die, and as obviously

it is good to live. That is not the issue here. The good which is the good use of knowl-edge is not alone the good of continuing to live, though it is good to live; and the evil which is the bad use of knowledge is not alone the evil of dying, though it is bad to die. The good which is the good use of knowledge is over and above any good to be found in nature, and the evil caused by the evil use of knowledge is far more blighting than the destruction of a world. We must face the fact that in such knowledge the good known may well be beyond the reach of mathematical and physical universals. Let us say it bluntly: the good of the good use of knowledge *is* substantially the good of eternal life; and the evil of the evil use of knowledge is eternal death. The man who decides not to blow up the planet because it is good not to do so — and note well that the good of not blowing it up is here not necessarily or only the good of survival, nor is the evil of deciding to blow it up only or wholly the evil of dying — that man is in principle already living forever. The same holds true for every sort of similar decision we make to use our knowledge well.

The good of deciding well, which is substantially eternal life, does not lie in knowing what we ought to do, nor even in knowing how to do things better than our forefathers. So to know what is good is, as we saw, like knowing a country only from knowing its map. Speculative knowledge of the arts and sciences is a good which remains intact even when we make bad use of that knowledge. Aristotle suggests that the deliberate solecism of a grammarian leaves the grammarian's *knowledge* of grammar unimpaired.[24] Just so, a high degree of medical art causes one to be a

good doctor, even if the doctor deliberately kills his patient; and the grammar of a
grammarian remains excellent even though
a grammarian is deliberately ungrammati-
cal. The Athenians, as you know, died like
flies of smallpox during the Peloponnesian
war for lack of medical art. We who know
medicine much better than they did, we
with our bacteriological warfare can do a
much better job than smallpox did. We
can wipe out whole civilizations. So too
with our planes, tanks, guns, A- and H-
bombs we can do a better job of man-
slaughter than the Macedonian phalanx or
the Roman legion. Clearly, the advance of
science and art may or may not further the
good of deciding well how to use science
and art. Science and art can thrive even
when men do not, and men can thrive
without art or science, though less well, by
deciding well how to use whatever knowl-

edge they have. Science and art have an instrumental or ministerial office in furthering the good of deciding well. A hungry, penniless wretch is not as likely to decide well how to use his knowledge as a man in easy circumstances. Now, easy circumstances can be caused by the advancement of the sciences of sociology, political economy, economics, etc. Yet the rich are not good men solely upon the score that they are rich. The good of the good use of knowledge is not the good of knowing necessary situations in nature, of knowing the ways out of, or among, or between those situations, though it is good to know all this. What, then *is* the good of deciding well?

A while back we saw that the knowledge of mathematicals and physicals enables us, not to change the necessary situations which science presents to us, but to face them, barter with them, weave our way in and out among them — but only up to the point of death. The good of deciding well is the good of changing the necessary situation according to which we shall all die, into a situation in which, despite death, we begin to live forever. Confronted by this good, the good of deciding well, we are face to face with the very heart of darkness. Yet in the heart of darkness we can hear the beating of light.[25]

Some pulsations of that light from that heart of darkness may now be indicated. It is clear that many men would rather die than deliberately choose what they know to be evil. Equally clear and unequivocal is our approval of their choice, even though we may not be up to their choice. *Dulce et decorum est pro patria mori.* This and similar adages are the very patrimony of mankind. Men know that to decide well is a greater good than any good which the choice of evil may bring them, even though it be the riches of Ormus and of Inde. Here we are faced with a fact, however the fact be explained: some men disdain their chances of survival when it is to cost them their honor, and we praise them for it. Now, even though they and we be mistaken in thinking that there is a good worth more than survival, nevertheless, this is a "mistake" which every man makes. Apparently, mistaken or not, we all have in us something or other which makes us fix our good above the goods of nature. This looks as though we are all in love with something not in nature.

Understand well this mysterious love of ours for something not in nature. And see, first, that love possesses the beloved in a way in which knowledge does not possess the object known. Secondly, see that this love, viz., the love for the good use of knowledge, possesses both nature and what is above nature. Yet that mysterious love of ours for the good use of knowledge is still knowledge.

In deciding to use our knowledge well we know a good which is greater than the good of survival, greater therefore than any good in nature; and it is in knowing this good, which transcends nature, *in that way*, viz., by deciding in favor of it, that we possess that good. A strange sort of knowing, this! A knowing which possesses the known, not by way of affirming the thing known, as we do in speculative sciences. "Two and two make four" we say, and go about our business enriched no doubt, but not enriched with any greater good than nature can supply. The discovery of the North Pole or of penicillin or of the relations of numbers and continuous quantities — speculative knowledge which is scientific — enriches us no doubt, but with what is already in nature and which becomes ours indeed by knowing it. And yet the knowledge of nature is the possession of nature only in the sense that such knowledge enables us to talk intelligently of nature. A superb ideal indeed. To talk intelligently of things — what could surpass this thoroughly Greek and therefore human goal? Only a different manner of possessing and a different goal as well. In knowing the good use of knowledge by deciding in favor of it we possess the object known only by wishing to possess it. It is ours for the taking, ours for having wished to possess it. A sort of knowing which is like, as Scripture puts it, "knowing one's wife." It is knowing which is loving. Surely this sort of knowing, knowing by loving, that is, falls not short of knowledge. It is a unique sort of knowing nevertheless, because it possesses the object which it knows by way of endowing us, because we so wish it, with the riches of the beloved. Speculative knowledge does not do this. Speculative knowledge, e.g., that $E = mc^2$, does not turn *us* into an atomic bomb. It turns us into *knowers* of a formula. Knowing by loving, however, does endow us with the riches of the beloved. A man who loves his wife possesses a good which is *his* good because *she* is his good, and the good which is she is now, by love, the good of the lover himself.

There is more to loving the good use of knowledge than that. Knowers of nature are, of course, in a much better situation than are natures, which know nothing. Yet knowers of nature do not quite transcend the natures they know. Knowers of nature are like the winner of a jackpot. It is good to win the jackpot. Observe, however, that the winner of the jackpot does not take more than is in the pot. Now, the lovers of the good use of knowledge are winners who take all. "I could not love thee, dear, so much, loved I not honor more," says the poet. Lovelace means that the love for a woman is stronger the more honor, which is greater than she, is loved. It is so. To love a person because one loves a good greater than a person is to love the person. No person can be loved without reserve — and so to love is the very nature of love, unless in loving a person we love a good which glows within a person and which is without reserve, and so is not alone the person loved. Thus, in "knowing one's wife" one knows much more than her, because in so knowing, much more is loved than she. What more?

We are now face to face with a state of

affairs, a truth, which if we know it by way of loving it, is the very peak of our liberty, and of our triumph over death, a way into the kingdom of God. This truth is a divine Person, and the way we know that truth or Person is by way of His free bestowal of Himself Who is Eternal Life and of our free acceptance of Him in an act of love.

No doubt God makes Himself known in the demonstration of God's existence. This point St. Thomas Aquinas has made clear by discerning that, since many exist-ents cannot exist upon the score that they are many — any more than many people can be sick because there are lots of them, therefore there must be a cause of many beings which cannot itself be many. He drew this demonstration — and in this he improved upon Aristotle's insight concern-ing substance, which insight of Aristotle's itself improves upon the mathematical and physical insights of science — he drew this demonstration from having seen that it is not because substance is the proper subject of the act of existing that it exists; rather because substance exists, therefore it is the proper subject of existing. With this fresh viewpoint of substance, St. Thomas could easily show that there is no reason in multiple substances which demands that they exist, even though they do. Hence, the reason why substances do exist must be God the Creator.[26] This demonstration no doubt enriches the mind, quite as any advance in knowledge does. More, it enriches the mind with an expectancy of good things which science cannot supply, and it does so in this way. Since God is the cause of the existence of things, He must exist in the sense that for Him to be God is for Him to exist. Since He is an act of existing, everything one

can say about Him must be by identity
that self-same act of existing. Now, one
can say about Him that He knows or is
intelligent, for He creates intelligent crea-
tures; and since to know is to be a person,
God is a Person. A Person, therefore pre-
sides over the universe, and the knowledge
that this is so is like the knowledge of
children that their father is in the house;
all is well.

And yet to know that God is a Person
by this formidable array of syllogisms, and
so to know that all is well is not quite
enough. We wish above all to know that
all is well *with us*, and to know that their
father is in the house is not particularly
consoling to many children. On the con-
trary. . . . Besides knowing that God is a
Person, we desperately need to know a
father in our love for him and in his love
for us. Of course, there would be no pos-

sibility of knowing a person in loving him unless we were somehow assured that a person exists. Nevertheless to know that a person exists even though that person be God Himself, is not yet to know Him as a lover.

It would only waste your time to demonstrate to you what you already know: our deepest human need is to love a person. From the criminal to the saint, with the in-betweens of fairly good to very good men, every manjack of us does whatever he does because he loves a person, himself or someone else. As Pascal remarks, even those who hang themselves do so because they think they are in a situation which is no longer tolerable to *them*. And Freud who put the very heart of all our goings on in *libido* said in a happier moment that he meant by *libido* pretty much what the English mean by "love."

St. Augustine perhaps expresses best of all our fundamental drive: *videre videntem,* to look upon one who looks back at us.[27] See it this way: a child whose father provides only food, shelter, clothing, and so on, is not well off. These are not the things a child wishes above all. Above all a child wishes to love and to be loved, and so do we grown-up children. A child wishes not only what a father can give but also the father himself — in his gifts if possible, but with or without his gifts, the father.

View this situation from both ends of it, from the lover's and the beloved's viewpoint. The beloved's gifts, if unaccompanied by the beloved's love, are like prey flung to an animal. An animal will pounce upon that prey, and so also would we, but whereas an animal is content with his prey, we are not. We want more than things which are flung at us, and we shan't be

well off until we have that more. That
"more" is the beloved in his gifts, his love.
Now, love is a free act: one which so issues
from the beloved's love for us that it could
have issued not at all. So for our love for
another. It too is a free act. Thus, we need
above all to pick up the beloved in his
gifts, and since we are free to let the beloved and his gifts lie, this is the supreme
gesture of freedom. In sum, all of us need
the free and gratuitous communication of
a person to a person, love freely offered
and as freely received, for this is the only
spot where spirits exult.

That there is such a spot as between
human beings is perfectly clear. Is there
such a spot as between man and God? The
indications that there is have already been
given.

Let us run through them once more.
Though men will not die for or without a

syllogism, some of them would rather die than live dishonored, and all of us praise them for it. What on earth could they be preferring here to life, what on earth could we be praising them for preferring to life? Surely they and we must think that it is better for them to die rather than to live dishonored. Now if they and we are mistaken about the matter, if, in other words, it is *not* better for them to surrender the whole world rather than suffer the loss of their souls, this is a mistake which love makes, the love for the good use of knowledge, and, we must add, it is a "mistake" which all men make. Surely all men cannot be wrong.

They cannot be wrong, not so much because there is a syllogism which demonstrates the existence of an eternal good which is God (though there is such a syllogism), but rather because the need men have for preferring death to dishonor is one with their need for being men. Let us see this in various ways. It is not because the good use of knowledge is commanded (though it is commanded) that it is good for us; rather the good use of knowledge is commanded because it is good for us: it answers our deepest need, viz., love. *We* demand the good use of knowledge. Men obey dictates of conscience, not so much because they are dictates, but because they love these dictates. Law, the dictates of conscience, the moral good, the good use of knowledge (all synonyms for our present purpose), all these are our allies, not because they have declared war along with us against the forces of evil (though they have declared war), but because we have wished them to be our allies; we have declared war first, and then we find law and so on to be on our

side. It is love which teaches us the good
use of knowledge, love, i.e., for that good
use of knowledge; it is not the other way
about: the good use of knowledge cannot
teach us to love it. There can *be* no good
use of knowledge unless we first bring that
use into existence by loving it. Love for
the good is first, and knowledge here is
love's disciple. We might see it this way:
even though by an impossible hypothesis
we were not obliged to follow the dictates
of the good use of knowledge, we know
that we should follow them nevertheless.[28]
Why? It begins to look as though we were
accomplices of law, not merely law's subjects. It begins to appear that we ourselves,
i.e., our love, are the middle term of the
demonstration that a good greater than
any good in nature lies within our good use
of knowledge. The syllogism might run
thus: whatever I cannot live without as

befits a man, I must have at all costs: now,
I cannot live as befits a man without the
good use of my knowledge; this, therefore,
I must have at all costs. The middle term
here "whatever I cannot live without as
befits a man," is ourselves, ourselves so
much in love with what befits a man that
we cannot do without it and be a man.
This invitation to be a man is an invitation to our freedom, an invitation to decide to be a man, or, alas, to decide not to.
Let that decision be made. As decision it
is knowledge still, but knowledge with a
difference. This is the knowledge which
frees.

For in that decision lies eternal life, or
death. In that decision a man begins to
live forever. For, the good which man cannot live without is often, by hypothesis, not
in nature. Often that decision is a surrender of the goods of nature. If then,

there be a God, it is He who is making the
advances to our free decision or love, to
accept Him in accepting the good use of
knowledge. And notice that the lover here
is eternal life. All lovers give themselves
and that is why we are enriched by those
we love. But human lovers can give no
more than themselves, and that is why we
shall not find eternal life in them. They are
not eternal life. God is eternal life, and
that is why in accepting Him by way of
accepting His invitation to stake our all
upon the good use of knowledge we begin
to live forever. As St. Augustine put it:
"You have made us unto yourself, and our
heart is restless 'til it rest in you."[29]

We have no right to expect the very
best scientific knowledge of mathematical
or physical universals to handle this situation between man and God. Science
handles necessary situations. This is a free

situation. And yet this free situation is one which confronts scientists also if not their science. After all, scientists love to know science, and that love of theirs for science is not their science. It is rather the initiation of their science. Had they wished to, scientists could have loved to be plumbers instead of studying science. As Einstein remarked, not too nostalgically I hope, he might have done better as a plumber. Moreover, even for scientists there is the problem of the good use of their science: whether they use their science well or ill, that is no skin off the nose of their science, though it is skin off their own noses. Their bad use of science makes scientists bad men, not bad scientists.

Nor is it any wonder that it is impossible to describe the consummation of the creature's love act for his Creator in the creature's love for the good use of his knowledge. It is impossible, not only because heaven is hard, and hell is easy, to talk about, but also because love has no words. The beloved within one's heart, what words can bespeak that presence! Eternal life lived now in loving One now Who is eternal life, here is a veil behind which only lovers dwell. Here the human lover knows a taste which is not upon the tongue, an odor which is not in the nostrils, a vision of the unseen. This lover exults though he may be racked with pain. This lover is hearing within himself the murmur of eternal waters returning to their source. Conversely, and now it is easy to talk about the matter, men who refuse to use their knowledge well suffer torment though they may be as healthy as mules and as rich as Croesus. Psychiatrists will confirm for us that the source of our deepest sickness is this: men will not deny themselves. Torment or joy, these are but the live tokens, the present foretaste of eternal life or death, because they are but God Himself either living within our free acceptance of Him in the good use of our knowledge, or absent in our refusal of the same. A mysterious situation indeed. A divine Person frantically signalling us through the good as we see it, to accept that good and in it Himself, or warning us that to reject that good is to reject Himself.

We might think indeed that the situation would be less strange if God offered Himself to our choice by way of being bared to our gaze and not through the screen of the good use of knowledge. Why should He not say to us, "take or leave Me," and not, as He does, "choose to use your knowledge well and with that you choose Me; or refuse to use your knowledge well, and in that refusal you refuse

Me?" The thing cannot be done. To see
God face to face — "This is eternal life to
know thee, Father, and Jesus Christ Whom
thou has sent" — to see God face to face is
to see Him Whom we can no longer reject,
and this is the consummation of our liberty, this is the prolongation of our freedom, the beatific vision. Yet the beatific
vision cannot be had unless we wish it;
and when we have it, we cannot not wish
it. There must, then, if the beatific vision
be the consummation of our liberty,[30]
there must be an obscure vision of the
good before there is the perfect vision of
it; the beggar maid, so to say, before the
queenly spouse. And if we are still inclined
to think that we are quite up to the job of
choosing the queen without her rags, we
are wrong on two counts. First, we are
forgetting that *we* are the beggar maid:
we presume. Secondly, we forget that,

beggarly as we are, the King cannot force our love for Him even in His splendor. He too, like any lover, tremblingly waits upon our decision, and that decision is so decisive that when made in favor of a crucified King it cannot fail to last forever.[31]

IV

I may conclude by restating our findings. The truth which sets men free is the truth of their knowledge. That knowledge is their knowledge of the arts and sciences which resides within their knowledge of using the arts and sciences well. Good knowledge well used, this seems to be the truth which frees men.

Good knowledge has two stages. First, the stage of the discovery of the necessary situations in nature. Secondly, the stage at which the speculative vision of the universal opens into the speculative vision of metaphysics. The step from the first to the second stage is made when one sees that the necessary situations in nature cannot be necessary upon the score that those necessary situations exist. There being no reason in nature why they exist, there must nevertheless be a reason, for those situations do exist. In other words, something which is necessary in being must exist, even though it be not those situations, for they are necessary only in essence. Thus the speculative vision of the universal opens into the speculative vision of God the Creator.

The discovery of the universal is the discovery of a "bit" of the necessary Being of God, and the demonstration of the existence of God leaves us, like blind and tongueless lions which have found water in the desert, drinking a draught we cannot taste or see. These two, the vision of the universal and the demonstration of the unknown God, seem to be the center and source, the joyful heart of speculative science's joy. No joy can surpass it, except only the joy of the vision of God Himself.

That the speculative joy of the scientist and of the philosopher may know no bounds, they have only to make the necessary Being which has swum into their ken under the wraps of His participated resemblances in the universals, or into the demonstrated proposition that He exists, they have only to make that necessary Being dwell in their hearts as men. This they can do by accepting the proposals He makes to their love to use their knowledge well.

The two sorts of knowledge, the speculative knowledge of the arts and sciences, and the practical knowledge of the good use of that speculative knowledge, can be so related as to destroy one or the other.

Here is a way of destroying speculative knowledge. A Catholic university which so understood the primacy of virtue, of the supernatural life, of faith, of the good use of knowledge, etc., etc., as to think these exclude the arts and sciences, a Catholic university which so understood the end of man as to be content with graduates who are, even *per impossibile*, ignorant saints, such a university would have ceased to be a university *and* Catholic at one and the same stroke. Let us remind ourselves that grace not only saves nature, but also heals it. To think that the sanative function of grace is unimportant because its salvific function is all important is nothing short of heresy. I cannot now do more with this point than remind you of it. We need the reminder. There have always been abroad those who have said that the sole end of

Catholic education is to teach a man to make an act of the love of God, and these same persons then go on to deplore the lack of Catholic scientists and artists. They might better have adverted to the fact that many Catholics who can make an act of the love of God cannot read or write, and so their complaint does not come well from them, for they have distorted the notion of education to start with by saying that the sole purpose of a Catholic education is to teach virtue. The distortion here is plain. No one can cause virtue by teaching. Besides, the cause of virtue, which is grace together with man's free cooperation with grace (*gratia Dei mecum*), is also the cause of the exercise of supernatural acts. Now, within exercised supernatural acts there are specifying features which come from nature. For example, a man decides to study and to use well the science of mathematics. Thus, mathematical knowledge and its good use get into existence, that is, into one's head and muscles, in virtue of a free decision. Not that wishing to know mathematics will get it known. That is nonsense. Rather, because wishing to know mathematics is, to date, the only known way of effectively (not specificatively) causing mathematics and its good use to be or exist; because the efficient cause is here the supernaturalized free act of man; because, lastly, within that now supernaturalized act of man there dwell *both* mathematics and, in the good use of mathematics, the secretly communicated good which is God — therefore a mathematician and his mathematics will live forever. So for any other sort of knowledge and the man who knows it. We cannot, then, seriously think that a Catholic university, or for that matter even the

Catholic Church, is interested only in saving men and not also in saving their minds. To think so is the sheerest theological and philosophical nonsense.[32] Let us have, as Sam Johnson would have said, no more of this nonsense.

I need not describe the way of destroying practical knowledge, because this whole lecture has failed if I have not made it clear why good knowledge should exist within the decision to learn and use good knowledge well.

The truth which makes men free would seem, then, to be the knowledge which is gained in deciding to make good use of our knowledge, and since the good gained by using knowledge well heals as well as saves human nature, good use of knowledge involves or strives to compass good knowledge itself. Note well these two components of the truth which sets us free:

the good *use* of knowledge, and good *knowledge* itself. The good use of feeble or false knowledge is no more an ideal freedom than is good knowledge badly used an ideal education. We are freest only when we decide to use *good* knowledge *well*. The truth which sets us free, then, is the honest-to-goodness truth we know about things in terms of the arts and sciences, but as dependent, in our good use of that truth, upon God.

NOTES

1. E. J. Drummond, S.J., Ph.D., *The Pursuit of Truth to Make Men Free*, Milwaukee, Marquette University Press, 1955; reprinted by the City News Publishing Company of New York in *Vital Speeches*, Vol. XXI, n. 22 (Sept., 1955), pp. 1466-1468.

2. Aristotle, *Metaphysics*, IX (Θ), 10, 1051b 7. So far as Sophism can be refuted, Aristotle makes the full-dress refutation of it in *Metaphysics*, IV (Γ), cc. 3-8.

3. Sometimes knowledge can cause a state of affairs, prudential and artistic knowledge, e.g., but that is not the question here.

4. Aristotle, *Metaphysics*, IV (Γ), 4, 1006a 1-1006b 35. Cf. *op. cit.*, V (Δ), 29, 1024b 19-21; *On Sophistical Refutations*, ch. 1, 164a 23-164b 25.

5. St. Thomas Aquinas, *De Veritate*, I, 10, corp.; *Summa Theologiae*, I, q. 17, a. 1; *In Metaph.*, V, lect. 22; VI, lect. 4.

6. . . . ὅμοιος γαρ φυτῷ . . ., Aristotle, *Metaphysics*, IV (Γ), 4, 1006a 15. St. Thomas Aquinas, *Summa Theologiae*, I-II, q. 51, a. 1.

7. W. James, *Psychology*, N.Y., Henry Holt and Co., 1892, p. 16. Aristotle, *Posterior Analytics*, II, 19, 100a 11.

8. Aristotle, *Posterior Analytics*, II, 19, 100a 11-13.

9. Aristotle, *Posterior Analytics*, II, 19, 100a 14 - 100b 5.

10. St. Thomas Aquinas, *Summa Contra Gentiles*, II, 83: The proper object of the intellect is being, as color is the proper object of sight.

11. St. Thomas Aquinas, *Summa Theologiae*, I, q. 86, a. 3. Vd. J. Owens, C.Ss.R., "The Intelligibility of Being," in *Gregorianum*, Vol. XXVI, n. 2 (1955), pp. 170-193.

12. Aristotle, *Categories*, ch. 5, 2a 11 - 2b 14.

13. Y. Simon, *Traité du libre arbitre*, Liège, Sciences et Lettres, 1951, pp. 33, 34.

14. The names of these two sorts of knowledge, viz., the knowledge of a subject in terms of its mathematical and physical predicates, and the knowledge of the subject in terms of its being, are, respectively, *perinoetic* and *dianoetic* knowledge. For a fuller explanation of these knowledges, see J. Maritain, *Dis-*

tinguer pour unir, ou les degrés du savoir, Paris, Desclée de Brouwer, 1932, ch. V, pp. 399 sqq.

15. Aristotle, *Categories,* ch. 5, 2a 11 - 2b 14.

16. Vd. Aristotle, *Physics,* III, 7, 207b 5; *Metaphysics,* VII (Z), 16, 1040b 5 - 10; X (I), 2, 1053b 16.

17. Plato, *Sophistes,* 244a - 260d, reluctantly came to the conclusion that sensibles demanded other sensibles, but then Plato thought that only his ideas were properly beings.

18. G. W. Leibniz, *On the Ultimate Origination of Things,* in *The Monadology and other Philosophical Writings,* Tr. R. Latta, N.Y., Oxford University Press, 1898, p. 338.

19. H. de Lubac, S.J., *Le Drame de l'humanisme athée,* 3e éd., Paris, Éditions Spes, 1945, pp. 351, 352, 152, 155 - 158. De Lubac is analyzing Dostoïevski's *L'Esprit souterrain.*

20. Aristotle, *Nicomachean Ethics,* X, 7, 1177b 31.

21. Plato, *Apology,* 30 ff.; cf. *Crito,* 54 ff., *Charmides,* 174 ff.

22. *John* xi. 25, in *The New Testament,* tr. Kleist and Lilly, Milwaukee, Bruce Publishing Co., 1954.

23. On the relation of intellectual to moral virtues see St. Thomas Aquinas, *Summa Contra Gentiles,* I, 4; III, 26; *De Virtutibus in Communi,* a 7; *Summa Theologiae,* I - II, q. 16, a. 6; q. 17, a. 6; q. 57, a. 1, *Resp.*; II - II, q. 166, aa. 1, 2; q. 167, a. 2; *In III Sent.,* d. 23, q. 1, a. 4, q. 1, *sed contra.* Vd. also E. Gilson, *Wisdom and Love in St. Thomas Aquinas,* Milwaukee, Marquette University Press, 1951, fn. 8, pp. 49 - 50; fn. 22, pp. 54 - 55.

24. Aristotle, *Nicomachean Ethics,* II, 4, 1105a 22 - 27. Vd. Plato, *Republic,* I, 340.

25. Dans le coeur la ténèbre, il [l'homme habitué à toujours monter et à trouver toujours] pressentira le battement de la lumière, A. de Valensin, S.J., *Regards* . . . , in the "Introduction d'Andre Blanchet," Paris, Aubier, 1955, p. 24.

26. On the demonstration of the existence of God, see G. Smith, S.J., *Natural Theology,* N.Y., The Macmillan Co., 1951, pp. 102 - 162. See also J. Owens, C.Ss.R., "The Causal

Proposition — Principle or Conclusion?" in
The Modern Schoolman, Vol. XXXII, n. 2
(Jan., 1955), pp. 159-172; 257-270; Vol.
XXXII, n. 4 (May, 1955), pp. 323-339.

27. Vd. S. Freud, *Beyond the Pleasure Principle*, cited by R. Dalbiez, *Psychoanalytical
Method and the Doctrines of Freud*, Vol. I,
tr. E. B. Strauss, N.Y., Longmans, Green and
Co., 1941, p. 175. St. Augustine, *Sermo LXIX*,
c. 2, 3; PL 38, 441: Hoc enim bonum est
videntem videre . . . Nobis autem promittitur
visio Dei viventis et videntis, . . .

28. Vd. J. Maritain, *Neuf leçons sur les notions
premières de la philosophie morale*, Paris,
Téqui, 1951, pp. 83, 84; H. de Lubac, S.J.,
Surnaturel, Paris, Aubier, 1946, p. 493.

29. St. Augustine, *Confessions*, I, 1, 1; PL 32,
661.

30. In St. Thomas Aquinas, *Summa Theologiae*, I, q. 62, a. 8, *ad*. 3, it is established that
there is greater liberty in the beatified angels,
qui peccare non possunt, than in us, *qui
peccare possumus*.

31. The lover's *yes* at the moment described in
the text is not just a nod to the good which

is God. It is like the plant's *yes* to the good of growing, fixing and totalizing all the plant's operations towards its end, the good of growing. Yet, unlike the plant's *yes*, a man's *yes* to the good of using his knowledge well, because it *freely* fixes and totalizes all his operations towards an end outside of nature, fixes and totalizes these operations forever. Thence the eternity of the good which a man wins by his *yes*. Thence also, since man and his operations are in time, the gradual growth of that eternal good within time. The eternal good has a history of only two moments: the moment of its inception, the moment of its complete fruition, which is the beatific vision. The in-between of that eternal good, i.e., its growth *in via*, is an in-between which is the very "substance of the things which do not appear." Yet those "things" are present in their very "now" which stretches from their inception to their full appearance. Within that stretch the eternal good is struggling to leaven the human paste until the whole man becomes leavened. This leavening process, this "eternalizing" of the whole of man and his operations, this divinizing of human nature, is not like the struggling of a cat in a sack. Rather (we must stick here to divine language), it is like the operation of leaven in the dough, silent, pervasive, powerful, working until the *whole* paste is leavened. When we step into heaven we shall flex and stretch ourselves like men who are at ease, because they are *in patria* — at home.

32. Cf. G. Smith, S.J., "The Position of Philosophy in a Catholic College," *Proceedings of the American Catholic Philosophical Association,* Vol. XXIX (April, 1955), pp. 20 - 40.

The Aquinas Lectures

Published by the Marquette University Press,
Milwaukee 3, Wisconsin

Fr. John Wellmuth, S.J., Chairman of the Department of Philosophy, Xavier University.

Cicero in the Courtroom of St. Thomas Aquinas (1945) by the late E. K. Rand, Ph.D., Litt.D. LL.D., Pope Professor of Latin, *emeritus,* Harvard University.

St. Thomas and Epistemology (1946) by Fr. Louis-Marie Régis, O.P., Th.L., Ph.D., director of the Albert the Great Institute of Mediaeval Studies, University of Montreal.

St. Thomas and the Greek Moralists (1947, Spring) by Vernon J. Bourke, Ph.D., professor of philosophy, St. Louis University, St. Louis, Missouri.

History of Philosophy and Philosophical Education (1947, Fall) by Étienne Gilson of the Académie française, director of studies and professor of the history of mediaeval philosophy, Pontifical Institute of Mediaeval Studies, Toronto.

The Natural Desire for God (1948) by Fr. William R. O'Connor, S.T.L., Ph.D., professor of dogmatic theology, St. Joseph's Seminary, Dunwoodie, N.Y.

St. Thomas and The World State (1949) by Robert M. Hutchins, Chancellor of The University of Chicago.

Method in Metaphysics (1950) by Fr. Robert J.

Henle, S.J., Dean of the Graduate School, St. Louis University, St. Louis, Missouri.

Wisdom and Love in St. Thomas Aquinas (1951) by Étienne Gilson of the Académie française, director of studies and professor of the history of mediaeval philosophy, Pontifical Institute of Mediaeval Studies, Toronto.

The Good in Existential Metaphysics (1952) by Elizabeth G. Salmon, associate professor of philosophy in the Graduate School of Fordham University.

St. Thomas on the Object of Geometry (1953) by Vincent Edward Smith, Ph.D., professor of philosophy, Notre Dame University.

Realism and Nominalism Revisited (1954) by Henry Veatch, Ph.D., professor of philosophy, Indiana University.

Imprudence in St. Thomas Aquinas (1955) by Charles J. O'Neil, Ph.D., professor of philosophy, Marquette University.

The Truth That Frees (1956) by Fr. Gerard Smith, S.J., Ph.D., professor and director of the department of philosophy, Marquette University.

First in Series (1937) $1.00; all others $2.00 Uniform format, cover and binding.